words of comfort
for Women

words of comfort

for Women

Carolyn Larsen

Revell

a division of Baker Publishing Group
Grand Rapids, Michigan

Published by Revell
a division of Baker Publishing Group
PO Box 6287, Grand Rapids, MI 49516-6287
www.revellbooks.com

Printed in the United States of America

Library of Congress Cataloging-in-Publication Data
Names: Larsen, Carolyn, 1950– author.
Title: Words of comfort for women / Carolyn Larsen.
Description: Grand Rapids : Revell, a division of Baker Publishing Group, 2019.
Identifiers: LCCN 2018055476 | ISBN 9780800736439 (pbk.)
Subjects: LCSH: Christian women—Religious life. | Bible—Meditations.
Classification: LCC BV4844 .L368 2019 | DDC 242/.643—dc23
LC record available at https://lccn.loc.gov/2018055476

20 21 22 23 24 25   7 6 5 4 3

Never Alone

So do not fear, for I am with you;
do not be dismayed, for I am your God.
I will strengthen you and help you;
I will uphold you with my righteous right hand.

ISAIAH 41:10

Fear, defeat, and hopelessness can make you feel alone. It may seem like no one understands how constant and oppressing your emotions are. Ugh. If only someone really got it and would just *be with* you. They might not be able to solve your problem, but you wouldn't feel so alone if someone was with you. A friend's presence would be such a comfort.

Here's some great news—you're not alone. Ever. God promised to be with you all the time. Not only that, he also promised to give you the strength to make it through all you're dealing with. He doesn't just show up when you have a problem; he's with you all the time. That means nothing takes him by surprise. So, when life gets messy and you feel like you can't hold on, keep putting one foot in front of the other. One day you'll realize that things are better. You'll realize that you made it because God was quietly walking beside you, and each time you needed a boost of strength, energy, or hope, he gave it. Each time you needed a spiritual hug or pat on the back, he gave it. His presence brings comfort, strength, hope, and perseverance just when you need it.

2

When You're Weary

Come to me, all you who are weary and burdened, and I will give you rest.

MATTHEW 11:28

You know what Scripture says . . . the ways that God instructs you to live in obedience to him and in community with others. Sure, you know. You do try to obey what Scripture teaches. But face it . . . living the Christian life is not a "one and done" thing. It's a journey. That means there are days of excellent success and days when you stumble. The longer you follow God, the more discouraged you feel when you fail to be obedient. After all, you don't want to disappoint God, and of course, you're trying your best. Your heart's desire is to truly live for him so that you become more and more like Christ.

What's God's response to your failures? Does he give up on you? Not at all! God understands the temptations and struggles you face. He knows that Satan constantly tempts you to turn away from God. He knows you need an oasis in the desert of temptation, and he offers himself as a place of comfort and rest. He invites you to come to him, so tell him what you're struggling against. Give it to him, and trust him to get you through it.

3

One Step at a Time

Set your minds on things above, not on earthly things.
COLOSSIANS 3:2

Worry, pray, worry, stress, worry, obsess, pray, stress . . . you know the cycle. Your mind locks onto something, and you can't think about anything else. So you worry, stress, and pray, then go right back to worrying and stressing. Why doesn't God do something? That's the million-dollar question. Is he paying attention? Yes. Doesn't he care about what's going on? Yes. Why doesn't he fix things? He will.

Recently a mother was angry on her child's behalf. Her son had been the victim of some very bad treatment and he was suffering emotionally. The mother obsessed about why God allowed this to happen. Why didn't he turn things around for her precious child? She was looking for answers and comfort from God.

Late one dark night, God spoke into that mom's heart: "Take comfort. I know that what's happened is hard, but it's just step one. There's more ahead." From then on, when worry threatened to overwhelm her, she focused her thoughts on God's promises. She remembered his love. She believed that he wasn't finished with the plans for her child's future. God's step-by-step plan brought her great comfort.

Never give in to despair; instead remember God's promises. Wait patiently for his step-by-step plan to develop.

4

Where Does Comfort Come From?

> *May our Lord Jesus Christ himself and God our Father, who loved us and by his grace gave us eternal encouragement and good hope, encourage your hearts and strengthen you in every good deed and word.*
>
> 2 THESSALONIANS 2:16–17

Sometimes life is just plain hard. A job loss, an investment failure, health issues, broken relationships, a prodigal child . . . and on and on. Some things are so painful that you may feel you simply can't make it and that this will be the thing that breaks you.

Your help, strength, and comfort will come from God. You know that. But the thing about God is that he won't force his way into your spirit or change your attitude. He will wait for you to ask for his help and comfort. Now, he may not take the problem away, but he will be right beside you as you go through it. He will guide you, strengthen you, teach you, and comfort you. It's important to pay attention to the ways God comforts you. His comfort may come through a calming of your spirit. It may come through a timely encouraging phone call from a friend or through a loved one simply sitting with you. Remember, especially in dark times, that God loves you. He wants to help you with the pain, loneliness, and stress of today and tomorrow. Call on him. He's waiting, and he will help.

5

Where's Your God Place?

I lift up my eyes to the mountains—
where does my help come from?
My help comes from the LORD,
the Maker of heaven and earth.

PSALM 121:1–2

The place where I feel closer to God than anywhere else is on the beach of any ocean he created. Sitting on the shore, staring out at the ocean with its lapping waves, sparkling water, leaping dolphins, and massive whales seems to put any problems I'm struggling with into perspective. I see the bigness of God in the bigness of the ocean.

I used to think I needed a special word from God in order to feel comforted. I wanted him to speak into my heart or make important words jump from my Bible's page to answer the problem causing my struggle.

One time I sat on a beach, thinking about a situation that was causing big-time angst and wishing God would just show me how he was solving the problem or at least how to get through it. Suddenly it dawned on me that the ocean's gentle waves were bringing me peace. The beauty of God's creation was giving me comfort. He had been speaking and comforting through creation; I just hadn't noticed it was him at first.

Where do you feel closest to God? Is there a place that gives you comfort just by its beauty or peacefulness? God's comfort can come in many ways. Don't dismiss the beauty around you—it may be his gift to you.

6

Remember

You make known to me the path of life;
you will fill me with joy in your presence,
with eternal pleasures at your right hand.

PSALM 16:11

Spiritual memory loss happens when you get so stressed out that you forget the times when God has been there for you in the past. You forget that he helped you through a crisis, gave you strength, comforted you . . . did everything he promises to do. The urgency of what you're currently facing washes away anything God did in the past. When you sink into the cycle of stressing, then forgetting, panic sets in. You have a desperate need for God to show up in some way.

Of course, God hasn't gone anywhere. He's still showing up in a multitude of ways—through a specific verse popping into your thoughts, a phone call from a friend, song lyrics, a beautiful sunset, a hug from a loved one—sending many reminders that you're not alone. He is always with you and nothing you face surprises him.

When you find yourself in the stress cycle . . . stop. Spend time reading Scripture and meditating. Pay attention to the positive things around you, and let your heart pull up memories of times when God worked in your life. Remember that he will do it again because, after all, he loves you!

7

Focused Thoughts

You will keep in perfect peace
those whose minds are steadfast,
because they trust in you.

ISAIAH 26:3

Most days, the news is filled with horrific things happening around the world. How are you supposed to rest in God's comfort when the world is filled with people and nations treating each other terribly? These situations can lead to some pretty depressing thoughts. Too often those thoughts plant themselves in your heart and mind, and it's hard to think about anything else. The result is fear and discouragement.

This verse in Isaiah is a key to experiencing victory over negative thoughts. While the answer to finding peace in all the ugliness is simple, it isn't always easy. Satan will fight against your effort to focus your mind on positive thoughts. How do you achieve victory? Stay in God's Word and let its message of love, forgiveness, and hope encourage your heart. Positive thoughts lead to more positive thoughts. Remember the ways God has cared for you in the past and how he has answered your prayers. If you steadfastly keep your mind centered on God, his Word, and the ways you've seen his hand in your life, then you will experience peace that can only come from him.

8

Living on a Hamster Wheel

Being confident of this, that he who began a good work in you will carry it on to completion until the day of Christ Jesus.

PHILIPPIANS 1:6

You've seen a hamster on its wheel—running like crazy but getting absolutely nowhere. Do you sometimes feel like one of those hamsters when it seems you're not making much progress in various areas of your life? Whether it's your spiritual growth, friendships, marriage, parenting, or career, sometimes you just feel stuck. You pray for God to show you how to move forward, how to improve, how to learn, how to grow . . . but it doesn't seem to be happening.

Never fear! God isn't finished with you yet. He will keep working in your heart and your life to move you forward. There will be times when you can't see any movement, but don't get discouraged. God's timing is always good. He waits for you to be ready for the next step in his plan or for someone else to be ready to receive what you'll bring to them. God knows exactly when to take you off the hamster wheel and put you back into action. Trust that he is still at work, even if you can't see it for a while. He has a plan—wait for it!

9

God Cares

Blessed are those who mourn,
for they will be comforted.
MATTHEW 5:4

Saying goodbye to a loved one is about the most painful thing humans must do. All you can think about is the person you lost. Grief is consuming, and getting past it takes time . . . in fact, you may never really get past it, but you somehow learn to live around it. What does it mean that God promises to comfort you in your grief?

It means that he cares about you. He cares that your heart hurts. God comforts you in different ways than he comforts others because he meets each person where they are. He walks slowly with you through the grief journey by speaking into your heart with precious memories of your loved one. Sometimes a funny memory makes you laugh out loud, or something simple, like a lovely flower or flock of geese overhead, reminds you that he's there. He reminds you that a believer's death is not forever and that you will be reunited with your loved one in eternity.

God understands grief. Love gives us strong connections with those we care about, and God understands that when those people are gone, we grieve. Because he loves you, he cares when you hurt.

10

The Reason for Grace

Let us then approach God's throne of grace with confidence, so that we may receive mercy and find grace to help us in our time of need.

HEBREWS 4:16

You want comfort? Well, friend, grace is the foundational part of your relationship with God, and it's what makes his comfort possible. Think about his grace for a moment. God's love for you is deeper and wider than any other love you know, and through his love he gives grace to you. Mercy and forgiveness are wrapped in that grace. Because of his deep love, he cares about you and wants to help you deal with life and grow deeper in love with him. He comforts you when you're hurting, holding you close and assuring you that one day everything will be okay. He comforts your heart when you're going through something that's difficult to understand or wondering why he doesn't make things better.

An amazing blessing of God's grace is that you have the privilege of talking with him about anything that's on your heart. Ask his forgiveness for your failures. Tell him what worries you have, and ask for guidance and direction. Ask him to care for your loved ones. Because of God's loving grace, you can confidently go to him; in fact, he invites you to.

Find comfort in his loving, grace-filled, compassionate heart, and trust that he cares.

11

Share the Burden

Cast your cares on the LORD
and he will sustain you;
he will never let
the righteous be shaken.

PSALM 55:22

You're struggling to carry several heavy bags of groceries—arms aching, things dropping—when suddenly someone grabs a bag from your hands and carries it for you. Your burden has been lifted! Heavy loads are so much easier when shared.

When you have a heavy burden of worries, God encourages you to give them to him. He will carry the load. Does that mean he takes the problem away? Does it mean he heals your sick loved one, gives you a new job, fixes a broken relationship, or brings back a wandering child? He may do those things . . . he also may not. What his offer to carry your load means is that he will be right there with you during the pain. He will give you the needed strength to keep on keeping on.

Why worry about things that your worry simply can't change? Tell God about the situation. Ask him to handle it, trust him to do so, and do your best to leave the problem with him and not grab it back to stress over. Allow him to give you the perseverance to get up each day, give the problem back to him (this may need to happen over and over), and trust him—again—to handle it. Your trust in his strength will keep you going.

12

Run to the Comforter

Come near to God and he will come near to you.

JAMES 4:8

When little ones have scary dreams, who do they go to? They run to Mommy or Daddy. When they are hurt and need some comfort, where do they go? Right, Mommy, Daddy, Grandma . . . someone who will comfort them and kiss the hurt away. They run to their comforter or cry out for the comforter to come to them.

Even adults need comforting sometimes, don't we? When your heart is so broken that you can't focus, when you're so scared about what could happen that you can't relax enough to sleep, when you're so confused about choices before you that your mind constantly races, where do you turn?

Just as a child cries out or runs to a trusted comforter, you have the offer before you to run to God for your comfort.

When you turn to him, he comes close to you. What does that mean? It's a heart thing—you sense his presence and comfort. You realize that you're panicking a little less and that your thoughts turn more often to how he has helped you in the past. You remember him.

13

A Safe Place for You

The LORD is my light and my salvation—
whom shall I fear?
The LORD is the stronghold of my life—
of whom shall I be afraid?

PSALM 27:1

When you have decisions looming and multiple choices each shouting that they are the best, you may be unsure which way to go. Never fear! You have a Way Maker who wants only the best for you. Ask God for guidance, and he will show you the choice that is his way for you. God's loving light will guide your life, comforting you in your struggle and protecting, teaching, and saving you. Will you make mistakes? Probably. But you can always go back to him and receive forgiveness and new, fresh light that reveals more of God's character, love, and guidance.

God is your safe place—that's what a stronghold is. He is your place of protection from danger, where you go to rest and find renewal of strength. He is safety and protection, light in the darkness, and comfort in the storm. He is your God. You can trust his heart of love for you even if you don't yet know what your next choice should be. Trust the Lord—your light and your stronghold. He will guide your heart and mind.

14

Nothing Surprises God

> *You have searched me, LORD,*
> *and you know me. . . .*
> *You discern my going out and my lying down;*
> *you are familiar with all my ways. . . .*
> *You hem me in behind and before,*
> *and you lay your hand upon me.*
>
> PSALM 139:1, 3, 5

Nothing catches God off guard. He never says, "Wow, I didn't see that coming." When life gets dicey, it's important to remember that nothing ever happens to you without God knowing all about it.

God doesn't have to scramble to figure out how to handle situations that pop up in your life. He doesn't have to search through his files to figure out what you need. God isn't like a repairman who says, "I'll come to your aid sometime between noon and five o'clock." His presence is immediate.

Psalm 139:5 reminds you that God has your back. In fact, he has you surrounded, so absolutely nothing happens to you or through you that he doesn't already know about. Satan can't get to you without God knowing about it. Trouble, enemies, illness—okay, he doesn't stop all the problems, but who knows how many things never actually come to pass because he is watching out for you? There are some things he must feel you can handle, but remember that he's got your back. He doesn't leave you alone to deal with those things. He's with you, offering strength, guidance, and comfort. Talk to him. Tell him how you're feeling. Ask for his help.

15

No "Elevator Speech" Needed

I love the LORD, for he heard my voice;
he heard my cry for mercy.
Because he turned his ear to me,
I will call on him as long as I live.

PSALM 116:1–2

Imagine you have the opportunity to speak with someone who has the power and authority to make positive changes in your world. Maybe that person is a government leader or the CEO of your company—someone who could implement policies that would improve the quality of life for a lot of people—and you have an opportunity for a few brief seconds to encourage that positive action. You would have to be ready with an "elevator speech." That's a short, concise, and to-the-point pitch, only about a minute long, covering the important issues you want him to hear. You spout your short speech, the powerful person hears it, and he goes on his way. You know that he probably gets many elevator speeches each day. Did he actually hear yours? Does he care about the issues you care about? Who knows?

Scenarios like that make you realize how very amazing it is that the Creator of all there is . . . the God of the universe . . . listens when you talk with him. He cares about what you say to him. He wants to know what concerns you have. You can talk to God anytime about anything. He wants you to!

16

Pass It On!

Praise be to the God and Father of our Lord Jesus Christ, the Father of compassion and the God of all comfort, who comforts us in all our troubles, so that we can comfort those in any trouble with the comfort we ourselves receive from God.

2 CORINTHIANS 1:3–4

God knows the problems you face. He sees your troubles. He sees the people who hurt you. You may know the reality that it is in the trenches of life's messes that your dependence on God grows the most. In that growth, you receive God's comfort through the grace of his love. God's comfort will help you through your difficulty, and it will help you learn more about faith as you move forward.

Here's the interesting thing though—the comfort and grace that God showers down on you is, of course, helpful, but it is not just for you. God expects you to receive his comfort and then pass that comfort on to those around you. You see, you're not in this life alone. No one is. You live, work, laugh, grieve, serve, and learn in community. People need other people in order to encourage, challenge, hold account-able, and comfort one another. Sometimes your comfort to another during a difficult time allows you the privilege of being "God with skin on" for them, which means he uses you to be the visible, practical reality of his love and comfort. God comforts you. You pass it on by comforting others.

17

Check Your DNA

Listen to me, you who pursue righteousness
*   and who seek the LORD:*
Look to the rock from which you were cut
*   and to the quarry from which you were hewn;*
look to Abraham, your father,
*   and to Sarah, who gave you birth.*
When I called him he was only one man,
*   and I blessed him and made him many.*

ISAIAH 51:1–2

Do you ever have days when you feel like you've totally blown it? Maybe it's a day when you've lost it with the kids big-time. Perhaps your impatience with your spouse reached epic levels today, or maybe the temptation to gossip about your friends overtook you. Whatever your "I blew it" moment stems from, it is discouraging. If you face these moments often you might even begin to question whether you're making any progress at all in your faith-walk. Does the question of whether you're even really a Christian float across your mind?

Hold on! Remember the rock from which you were cut. Remember the quarry that rock came from. What does that mean? It means that your heritage goes all the way back to Adam and Eve, who were created in God's image. This means that you were also created in his image. Your DNA proves that you are God's child. It's his DNA in your soul. Even if you blow it time after time after time, you're still God's child. It's still his DNA in you. Each of your failures is followed by his forgiveness and grace and is another chance to live for him!

18

Stop, Pray, Wait

"I know the plans I have for you," declares the LORD, *"plans to prosper you and not to harm you, plans to give you hope and a future."*

JEREMIAH 29:11

One certainty in life is change. Sometimes you think you're settled in for the long haul, then something happens that's out of your control and changes everything. A job loss, a broken relationship, a cross-country move, illness, the death of a loved one . . . change is inevitable. Change can leave you standing at a crossroads with uncertainty regarding which path to follow. Maybe there's more than one good option. Maybe there's one you really want to take, but you're just not sure it's right. What do you do?

Stop, pray, wait. Read Scripture, and don't rush into a decision. Just *be* for a while, and give the Holy Spirit a chance to guide your heart. God has a plan for your life, so he has an opinion about which path you should take. Give him a chance to reveal that plan to you. If you have to start moving forward, bathe every step in prayer. Pay attention to opportunities God opens for you and to how you feel about them. God will guide you.

Take comfort in the fact that God knows what he's doing. He sees a bigger picture than you can see, and he will guide your path.

19

Honest Trust

The LORD is good,
a refuge in times of trouble.
He cares for those who trust in him.

NAHUM 1:7

You've seen circus performers who climb onto swings high in an arena. Two performers swing toward each other, one hanging by the knees. The second flings herself from her swing and trusts the first one to catch her and keep her from falling to the floor.

Trust. It's not easy. How are you at trusting God? Trust evokes an uneasy feeling that you may not often think about—the feeling of letting go of control. When you trust God to take care of you . . . to catch you before you fall . . . you are letting go of your own power in a situation. You're not in control anymore. That's when the honesty of your trust in God becomes an in-your-face reality—more than just words; it becomes actual submission to God. Your complete trust in

God shows whether you truly believe his love and care for you. It shows that you trust he is paying attention. It shows you believe he has a plan and that he is moving you forward in that plan. It shows that you trust him with your life and all those you love, to the point that you will follow wherever he leads. Trust God. He loves you more than you could ever know!

20

Jesus Wins!

I have told you these things, so that in me you may have peace. In this world you will have trouble. But take heart! I have overcome the world.

JOHN 16:33

What an awesome promise! Jesus has overcome the world. No matter what's going on or how tough life is—Jesus wins! Hopefully you find great comfort in this verse. Our world is a pretty chaotic place these days. In our current culture, too many people feel comfortable making comments that are brutal and just downright mean, and it doesn't seem to matter to them whether the stories they comment on are true or whether they have all the facts. Public figures who are on social media and who share comments that are unkind, judgmental, and cruel have contributed to this.

All of this can cause you to feel attacked because of your own beliefs. Those attacks make you feel alone and even ostracized by some friends and family. Some people have lost the ability to be kind to those who disagree with them. So, how do you respond?

Be true to yourself and to your trust in God. Spend serious time in Scripture so the Holy Spirit can guide your thoughts, beliefs, actions, attitudes, and responses. Put your trust in God to deliver you through difficult times. And hang on . . . Jesus wins! He has overcome the world!

21

Covered in Prayer

The Spirit helps us in our weakness. We do not know what we ought to pray for, but the Spirit himself intercedes for us through wordless groans. And he who searches our hearts knows the mind of the Spirit, because the Spirit intercedes for God's people in accordance with the will of God.

ROMANS 8:26–27

We often spend prayer time telling God what we want him to do for us. Of course he wants to hear our prayers, and he understands that we generally want things to go our way, so we hope that our will is his will too. However, no doubt there are times when you simply don't know how to pray. You don't know what would be best for all involved. You don't know how to ask God to fix the situation. You want to pray, but you just don't know what to say.

That's when the Holy Spirit steps in. He sees your heart and knows what your desires are. Because he is also God, he sees into the future and knows what's best for the situation. So, knowing the will of God and knowing your heart, the Holy Spirit speaks a prayer to God on your behalf about the situation.

If you can't find the words to pray—if you aren't even sure how you want a problem to be solved—trust the Holy Spirit who sees the end from the beginning. He will speak on your behalf, and you can rest in the knowledge that the situation will be covered in prayer.

Your Strong Anchor

God did this so that, by two unchangeable things in which it is impossible for God to lie, we who have fled to take hold of the hope set before us may be greatly encouraged. We have this hope as an anchor for the soul, firm and secure.

HEBREWS 6:18–19

A ship depends on its anchor to keep it tethered to one spot. Regardless of the wind or waves, the anchor's job is to hold the ship steady.

Jesus is the anchor for your soul. Through all the storms life throws at you, he will hold your soul tightly. What kind of storms do you face in life? Broken relationships? A job ending? Financial stress? Prodigal children? Illness? The storms of life are multitudinous. They are different for everyone. Some people face the loss of their homes from natural disasters. Some live through war, drought, hunger, and poverty. There's no doubt—life can bring difficult, painful situations.

How does Jesus anchor your soul in difficult times? By giving you strength to simply make it day-to-day. He reminds you that God loves you, no matter how tough life is. He reminds you that nothing is more important than your relationship with God and that you should hold tightly to him. Jesus keeps you focused on God and gives you the perseverance to trust him. Does this mean he doesn't care about the troubles you face? Of course he cares. He walks through them with you. You're never alone.

Faith Lessons in the Dark

> Even though I walk
> through the darkest valley,
> I will fear no evil,
> for you are with me;
> your rod and your staff,
> they comfort me. . . .
> You anoint my head with oil;
> my cup overflows.
>
> PSALM 23:4–5

Total darkness is unnerving at best and terrifying at worst. In a total blackout you still instinctively strain to see where you're going, but you can't even see your hand in front of your face. You can't see where you're going. You can't see what's around you. You can't see what's coming toward you.

Trying to walk in such darkness might mean you run into things or even hurt yourself. It's dangerous to try to move about when you can't see anything. But what if someone was beside you, guiding your steps, directing you around dangerous places? Even if you couldn't actually see your guide, you would depend on his help, right? Well, you do have a Guide. God is there. Even though you can't physically see him, he's right beside you, guiding your steps and protecting you on the journey. He calms your fears and comforts your heart.

When you're maneuvering through the dark times of life, that's when the rubber meets the road with your faith. It's when you find out if you trust God enough to step out in the darkness and let him guide you forward. Lessons learned in the dark are the most life-changing lessons. Start moving. Trust your Guide in the darkness.

Share Your Story

If we are distressed, it is for your comfort and salvation; if we are comforted, it is for your comfort, which produces in you patient endurance of the same sufferings we suffer. And our hope for you is firm, because we know that just as you share in our sufferings, so also you share in our comfort.

2 CORINTHIANS 1:6–7

Reading or hearing the story of someone who has endured a painful, frightening situation and persevered through it is inspiring. You begin to see that if that person can go through such a terrible time and come out in one piece, then you can face your problems and have victory over them. You gain strength from hearing others' stories and especially from seeing how God cared for them through it all.

The apostle Paul knew about the power of stories. He shared his stories of persecution and suffering in the Bible so you could learn from his experiences and be encouraged. Through reading how God cared for Paul and other Bible characters, you learn that he will also take care of you. You see that God didn't always take away people's troubles. He didn't always solve the problem, but he stayed beside them, supporting and strengthening them every day. Those stories help you to see his character and his heart through the words of Scripture. So, read those stories and learn from them. Then share your stories to help others, and listen to their stories to gain encouragement yourself. Tell others how God cares for you, and challenge them to reach out to him too.

25

Pursued!

> *Surely your goodness and love will follow me*
> *all the days of my life,*
> *and I will dwell in the house of the LORD*
> *forever.*
>
> PSALM 23:6

eing pursued can be a bad thing or a good thing. Being chased by someone who means you harm? Bad. Being chased by other participants in a race? Good. Being pursued by a potential boyfriend? Well, that could be bad or good; it depends. Being pursued by a college recruiter or a potential employer is good, and being pursued by someone who wants the very best for you and refuses to let you settle for less is very good!

Think about it—God won't let you give up on your life with him. He loves you too much to allow you to walk away. Even if you get discouraged and want to give up when problems come and you don't believe God is paying attention to your prayers, he will pursue you. Even if your own choices pull you away from God, he will show you how much he loves you. There's nothing you can do that will change that. God will never say, "I've had enough of you" and walk away. You can trust God to pursue you through your apathy, through your pain, through your discouragement. Pay attention to the ways God reaches out to you. Pay attention to his pursuit. Stop running from him, and start running toward him.

Strength Together!

Encourage one another and build each other up, just as in fact you are doing.

1 THESSALONIANS 5:11

Our screen-obsessed culture has contributed to the destruction of face-to-face conversations and in-depth relationships. The interesting thing is that while people can be constantly connected with others through social media, there is a reported epidemic of loneliness in our culture. Apparently the screen connections do not lead to true, in-depth friendships.

Face-to-face conversations provide good opportunities to build honest relationships where you can encourage others. As you see your friend's facial expressions and hear the tone of her voice, you get a better idea of how she's really feeling than you can from seeing her words on a screen.

God created people to live in relationship so that we can encourage one another to become the best people we can be. When you work side by side with others, you become good servants of Christ. Life is pretty lonely if you don't have friends to help carry the burdens of hard times or to celebrate the good times. You can find comfort through relationships and give comfort to others. When we encourage and build each other up, we share in each other's ministries, joys, and sorrows. Think of it like the Red Rover game from your youth—hands tightly joined in strength, helping each other resist whatever life brings!

27

A Safe Place

God is our refuge and strength,
an ever-present help in trouble.
PSALM 46:1

Sometimes you need a safe place to hide, a place where your enemies can't get close. Thankfully, you have that. God is your refuge, your safe place of protection. When you retreat to him, you trust him to keep you safe, and he does! He covers you and hides you from your enemies, so you can settle in and rest your tired and anxious heart while you wait for him to direct your next steps.

Being hidden away in God's refuge is important because while you're there he will refresh you and renew your strength. He will whisper his presence into your heart and help you to continue moving forward. Then when you are ready to leave your hiding place, you are more prepared to face your life again—including the enemies who continue to attack you.

The comforting thing is that you can hide in God as often as you need to. He is always there, ready to take care of you and give you the strength you need. Regardless of what's going on in your life, God is paying attention and is ready to help.

28

Work in Progress

Not that I have already obtained all this, or have already arrived at my goal, but I press on to take hold of that for which Christ Jesus took hold of me.

PHILIPPIANS 3:12

Good things are worth waiting for and, let's face it, sometimes good things are a long time coming. As a teen, you waited to get your driver's license, or to finish school and start your career, or maybe even for Mr. Right to come along. As an adult, maybe you've waited through the process of pregnancy or even to be able to get pregnant. Maybe you've endured the waiting that goes along with the efforts to lose weight.

Does it seem like growing a mature faith in God takes a long time? Well, it does. A life of faith is often called a journey because it's a learning process. There are times of growth and then times of regression. Sometimes a moment of a bad choice, an uncontrolled reaction, or a selfish insistence makes you feel like you're never going to get there.

But take comfort in the truth that you will! If, in your heart, you desire to know God, to live for him, and to honor him, Jesus won't let you go. He is holding you, and he will keep teaching you and guiding you into the best person you can be. Don't get discouraged—he's not done with you yet!

29

The Wisdom You Need

If any of you lacks wisdom, you should ask God, who gives generously to all without finding fault, and it will be given to you.

JAMES 1:5

It's interesting that this verse says *if* you lack wisdom; it seems like *when* would be more realistic. Every person needs help with wisdom from time to time. God sees that your heart's desire is to live for him, honoring him with your life, actions, words, and attitudes. He also sees that there are times when it's hard to do those things in a way that communicates love and care for others as you honor him. When that happens, ask God for wisdom to guide your actions and your words. You needn't worry that your request communicates failure. It doesn't. It communicates dependence on him. You can trust that God wants to help you grow deeper in love with him. He wants to help you live in wisdom so that, by the way you live your life, you make faith in him something others will also want to know.

What a blessing it is that you can ask God for wisdom without worrying that he will chide you or be disappointed with you. He knows your human frailness and he sees your heart of longing. He will give you the wisdom you need today and tomorrow and every day after that.

30

Greatest Love

Greater love has no one than this: to lay down one's life for one's friends.

John 15:13

"Jesus loves me, this I know, for the Bible tells me so." We're all familiar with these lyrics, and they are proof of how much Jesus loves you. This chapter's opening verse is often quoted in recognition of Jesus dying for your sins, which, of course, is the ultimate example of a life laid down for you.

But there's another element of Jesus's gift—he willingly left the glory of heaven and came to earth to live as a human being. He set aside his heavenly residence so that you would know that he understands the challenges, difficulties, struggles, and blessings of being human. He can empathize with your struggles because he has lived them. He continues caring for you by his daily forgiveness of your sins and his day-in and day-out provisions for you.

Jesus's love for you is great. Look at the evidence: Jesus left heaven for you. Through his teachings while he was on earth, he gave you guidance for how to live. He suffered and died for you. These provide clear proof that he cares for you. No matter how difficult life gets, do not ever doubt his care—look at how much he has already done for you!

31

Never Shaken

> *"Though the mountains be shaken*
>   *and the hills be removed,*
> *yet my unfailing love for you will not be shaken*
>   *nor my covenant of peace be removed,"*
> *says the LORD, who has compassion on you.*
>
> ISAIAH 54:10

An earthquake will totally change the contour of the earth where the tremor happens. Mountains fall. Valleys and gorges are created. Trees come down. Buildings crumble. You've seen the changes made by earthquakes. Nothing in that landscape will ever be the same again. People who live where an earthquake strikes have to live with a new normal. They have to rebuild their homes and adjust to the ways their lives have changed. Like quakes that shake the earth, unexpected events can cause upheaval in our lives.

Have you had an earthquake in your life? It could come in the form of a divorce or the death of a spouse or someone you're close to. It changes everything about your life. Your landscape is different. There are multitudes of other ways that the landscape of your life can change. A financial crisis changes your life completely. A job loss is a major change.

God promises that whatever earthquakes shake up your life, there is one thing that won't crumble. His love will not be shaken. No storm or problem will make it fall away. Grab on to him when life gets hard. Hold on tight. He promises his love and peace. God may not stop the earthquakes or storms of life, but he will never desert you during them. His compassion will surround you.

32

A Lighted Path

Your word is a lamp for my feet,
a light on my path.

PSALM 119:105

Children have the coolest shoes. Many styles have lights in the sides that flash as the wearer runs and jumps. Too bad adults don't get light-up shoes. Wouldn't it be helpful to have little headlights in the toes of your shoes so you can see the path ahead of you and know if there are things that might trip you up? When you can see what's coming, you can make the necessary adjustments to avoid something that could make you fall.

God, in his great compassion, has already provided you a way to know what's ahead and a way to be prepared for anything that comes. His Word tells you everything you need to know about the struggles that could be ahead for you and how you can be prepared for them. The Bible teaches you how to have a deep relationship with God so that his strength and power flow through you.

God wants to help you be prepared for life. He knows that the most important thing you can learn is to depend only on him. Knowing him deeply and obeying him completely are the keys to comfort and peace, and knowing God's Word is the pathway to that relationship.

33

Stop the Noise

Be still, and know that I am God;
I will be exalted among the nations,
I will be exalted in the earth.

PSALM 46:10

It's quite possible your mind is constantly moving, multi-tasking between each of the things you need to accomplish today: caring for those who are ill; serving others; being there for family members who need you; tending to work responsibilities, chores you need to do, and church stuff; reading books you want to read; catching up with friends you miss . . . a bazillion things can run through a woman's mind in a matter of minutes, right? Some stick, and you chew on them for a while. Some shout for attention. The point is that all those thoughts keep your mind occupied. So, even as you beg God for comfort and grace, even as you ask him for hope and peace, how are you going to hear his voice?

He says to "be still." Quiet your thoughts. Stop activity. Sit. Be. Give your tired spirit and worn-out mind a chance to hear what God wants to say to you. He will speak, but he won't shout through the noise. Make time with him your focus for even a few minutes a day, and just listen.

34

Cut the String!

Cast all your anxiety on him because he cares for you.
1 PETER 5:7

Cats love to play with toys. It's fun to watch a cat bat around a little toy, pounce on it, bat it again. Some toys have an attached string so you can toss the toy toward your cat then slowly pull it away as the cat prepares to pounce. It's a game of cat and mouse—near capture by the cat, escape by the toy. It's a fun interaction between you and your pet but not so fun when it defines how you interact with God.

Your loving Father invites you to give your worries and cares to him. He extends this invitation because he loves you and he wants to lighten your load. He wants to handle life for you. Don't take this offer lightly; he means it. He loves you that much.

Maybe you do give God your worries and cares. Maybe you ask him to free you from anxiety. Maybe you *mean* to mean it . . . but you keep that string attached to your worries so you can pull them back and own them yourself again. There's no peace in that, no way to gain comfort. Cut the string. Give your anxiety to God, and trust him to handle your problems.

35

Growing Up

When you pass through the waters,
I will be with you;
and when you pass through the rivers,
they will not sweep over you.
When you walk through the fire,
you will not be burned;
the flames will not set you ablaze.

ISAIAH 43:2

When you accept Christ as your Savior, you are born into new life with him. That's how we describe the beginning of someone's Christian walk—as new life. After you were physically born, you went through the growth progress of crawling, standing, walking, drinking milk, eating baby food, then eating real food. It was a process.

New life in Christ can be viewed in the same way. As you learn to trust God with small things, you see his care and guidance. Then it's a bit easier to trust him with something a little bit bigger, and again, you see his care and guidance. As you recognize God's faithfulness, you learn to trust him no matter what life brings. But, you must start somewhere.

Are you carrying worries that you just have not been able to let go of? Are you unwilling to give your concern to God because you're unsure he will actually handle the problem or at least hold your hand as you wade through it? He will. But you have to give him the opportunity. Ask for his help with a small worry to start, then see his care and let the growth process of trusting faith take hold in your heart.

36

Deal with Today

Do not worry about tomorrow, for tomorrow will worry about itself. Each day has enough trouble of its own.

MATTHEW 6:34

Imagine you have five water glasses. One is full of water and the others are empty. The full glass represents today—the water in it, your worries and cares for *this* day. If you pour some of today's water into the glass for tomorrow, you might think you're lightening today's cares. In reality you're making tomorrow's cares worse because that day is going to have enough cares to fill its own water glass.

Are you guilty of shooting ahead to worry about tomorrow or next week or a year from now? You are worrying about things that may never happen. Do you fixate on what might happen or what could come to pass? It takes so much energy to worry. That energy output means you don't have the energy you need to deal with today's cares and worries.

In fact, any worry at all is a waste of energy. Worry won't change a thing; however, it is a very human response to the stresses of life. Don't stress about worrying, but take one day at a time. Don't leap ahead. Give today to God, and ask him to relieve your worry and handle your cares.

37

Trusting in Prayer

Do not be anxious about anything, but in every situation, by prayer and petition, with thanksgiving, present your requests to God.

PHILIPPIANS 4:6

Don't be anxious? How can God even suggest that? Doesn't he know how difficult it is to eliminate anxiety from your life? Seriously, is it even possible? It's a goal to have, right? It should be, because letting go of anxiety means replacing it with trust in God.

God wants to comfort, strengthen, and protect you by hearing your concerns through your prayers. You can tell him what's stressing you. You can tell him what worries are pulling on your heartstrings.

What stops you from praying instead of worrying? Do you trust in the power of prayer? Do you believe God hears your prayers . . . that he wants to hear them? Don't give the answer you know you're supposed to give. Think about it. Do you honestly trust God to hear your prayers and to answer them?

Have you seen God's care through answered prayers for yourself or others? Have you seen his hand in your life? If you've seen it once, you'll see it again. Take your cares to him. Thank him for his answers before you even see them. Your faith will grow as you receive his comfort and care.

38

Surviving the Fire

Because of the LORD's great love we are not consumed,
for his compassions never fail.
They are new every morning;
great is your faithfulness.

LAMENTATIONS 3:22–23

Wildfires are terrifying. They roar across the country-side, consuming everything in their wake. Forests, fields, vineyards, and yes, homes are destroyed by the power of those massive fires. The destruction left behind is a good definition of "consumed." Nothing is left. Everything is gone . . . destroyed.

Perhaps there have been times when you have felt that you were going to be consumed by the struggles of your life. These situations you face seem hopeless. They appear too massive for you to work through. It feels like you take one step forward and four steps backward in your efforts to get your head above water. "God," you cry, "I'm losing the battle here. This thing is winning. Help me!"

You've done the right thing—you've called on God for help. His love for you is so complete, so unconditional, so deep that he will keep you from being consumed by the struggle. You will not be destroyed. You may be bruised, you may be exhausted, but you will survive. Every single day, God's mercy and compassion cover you. He never fails.

39

Parenting Struggles

Start children off on the way they should go,
and even when they are old they will not turn
from it.

PROVERBS 22:6

How's your parenting experience going? Are you concerned about your child's rebellion or stubbornness? Has your child turned his back on God and on everything he's been taught? Does it seem like everyone else has perfect children while you're in a constant battle with your child? Do you feel that the bulk of your prayers are over this child? Yeah, it's tough. Contrary to what you may have expected, parenting gets more stressful—not less—as your children grow.

You pray that your children will grow up to be good adults who walk with the Lord and who are kind and considerate. But what if things aren't going that way? Then find comfort in this promise from God. The seed is planted. You've made certain that your child knows about the Lord and has been exposed to the blessings of faith. Trust God that at some point your child will return to him. You've laid the groundwork. Keep praying. Keep modeling a life of faith. Believe God's promise. He won't let go of this child you love so deeply. You may not get to see the return or even know about it. It's between your child and God. So, just keep trusting.

40

God's Goals for You

Though you have made me see troubles,
*   many and bitter,*
*   you will restore my life again;*
from the depths of the earth
*   you will again bring me up.*
You will increase my honor
*   and comfort me once more.*

There's a bigger picture to your life than what's happening today. There's a greater goal than your happiness and comfort in this moment. While that may be hard to accept, especially if your today is loaded with difficulty and struggle, it's important to remember. God's goals for you are more in-depth than your momentary happiness.

From the first moment you accept Christ as your Savior, God has a plan to grow your heart so that you look more like Jesus. That growth doesn't happen while you're sitting on a couch eating bonbons. It takes work. Just as an athlete trains for hours and hours until their body cries out for relief, your spiritual growth will be intense. It will take you through difficult times of pain and stress. There will probably be times when you feel you can't go on. But, you will because God doesn't leave you alone in the hard times.

When life gets difficult, look for God. See which of your spiritual muscles he is training: Trust? Obedience? Humility? Something is going on; you can be sure of that. Take comfort in the fact that he cares enough to grow you to be more like Christ.

41

Dependable Trust

Know therefore that the LORD your God is God; he is the faithful God, keeping his covenant of love to a thousand generations of those who love him and keep his commandments.

DEUTERONOMY 7:9

Trust. It takes a long time to truly trust another person. You have to get to know a person to see their character, understand their heart, and come to believe that this person is a trustworthy friend. Then you know you can trust them to keep your confidences, to always have your back. You can trust them to be honest and forthright with you. A trustworthy friend is a gift from God.

But what happens when a friend breaks your trust? It takes a long time to rebuild, doesn't it? Sometimes you feel you can never completely trust that person again. You never reach that level of relationship again.

Hopefully you have spent time getting to know God and learning to trust him. You don't have to be concerned about him betraying your confidence. He can be trusted—always. He has kept his promises for thousands of years, and that's not going to change now. Don't expect him to act outside of his character or his Word. Know him. Know his Word. Believe his love. Trust his faithfulness.

Your Song

> *The LORD your God is with you,*
> *the Mighty Warrior who saves.*
> *He will take great delight in you;*
> *in his love he will no longer rebuke you,*
> *but will rejoice over you with singing.*
>
> ZEPHANIAH 3:17

Has anyone ever dedicated a song to you or maybe posted a song in your honor on social media? When another person thinks enough of you that a song seems appropriate, it's pretty special, isn't it? Or when someone loves you so much that they burst into song to tell the world about you and celebrate the "youness" of you.

It's even more special that God, the Creator of all there is, celebrates you with a song! He saves you, pulls you into his fort of protection, and loves having you there. Then, he—God himself—is so happy you're there that he sings a song over you.

What do you imagine that song is about? It celebrates his deep, deep love for you. He sings of how he pulled you back from the brink of destruction and settled you safely in his protection. He tells how wonderful you are . . . how special you are to him . . . how he's thrilled that you chose to give your heart to him. He promises to always care for you, comfort you, guide you, and protect you. His song is of love for you and dreams for your future. How awesome is that?

43

This Is Love

This is how God showed his love among us: He sent his one and only Son into the world that we might live through him. This is love: not that we loved God, but that he loved us and sent his Son as an atoning sacrifice for our sins.

1 John 4:9–10

Do you see the depth of God's love for you? He didn't *have* to do anything for you. He didn't *need* you to love him. He didn't need you in his heaven. But he held nothing back from you. He sent his most precious Son to earth to teach humankind about himself and to encourage people to give their hearts to him. God allowed his Son to be tortured and murdered so he could take your sins on himself. Jesus paid the price for those sins so that you could have a way to know God. All barriers between you and God were destroyed, and a bridge was created so that you could come to him.

If God didn't need you to know him or to be in his heaven, then why did he go to all this trouble? One simple reason: love. And not just his love for the whole of humankind or for the "good people" around you—he loves you. Day in and day out, God loves you. Whatever is happening in your life today, God loves you. Nothing can ever change that. God loves *you*.

44

Forever Love

I am convinced that neither death nor life, neither angels nor demons, neither the present nor the future, nor any powers, neither height nor depth, nor anything else in all creation, will be able to separate us from the love of God that is in Christ Jesus our Lord.

ROMANS 8:38–39

People come and go. Some people are in your life for only a season and when that comes to an end, the relationship drifts apart. Some relationships end because they are broken into a million pieces and you can't even be civil with each other anymore. Friends, boyfriends, spouses, co-workers—no relationship is forever. Even if it lasts through life, death will eventually break it. All relationships end except one—your relationship with God is forever. Nothing can ever separate you from his love.

You may have times when it feels like you aren't connecting with God. He seems to be silent, and it feels as though your prayers do not go beyond the ceiling. Has he turned away from you? Is he tired of your disobedience or your failures? Have you disappointed him one too many times? Those dark times are not fun, but God does not walk away from you.

No, God's love for you is so deep and strong that nothing on this earth can break it. In fact, not even death will break it. No matter what you're dealing with today, take comfort in God's deep love for you. His love is yours forever and ever.

45

The Reason to Go On

You turned my wailing into dancing;
*   you removed my sackcloth and clothed me*
*   with joy,*
that my heart may sing your praises and not be silent.
LORD my God, I will praise you forever.

PSALM 30:11–12

When you're grieving the death of a loved one, it feels like that pain and sense of loss will never end. You can't imagine how you're going to go on without that person in your life. Or when a marriage explodes into divorce—a divorce that you didn't want—the pain is so sharp and deep you can barely find a reason to get out of bed each day. Will you ever feel better?

Ask God to take away your pain and replace it with joy. Ask him to heal your heart. Step-by-step, you will begin to find a way to go on. One day you will find yourself smiling at something and realize it's been a long time since you smiled. Soon you will anticipate going out in public, being with friends, and helping others who are going through hard times. You will be willing to give of yourself again.

How does this change come about? Through God's gentle comfort and care upholding you, loving you, and helping you see the sunshine instead of the clouds. Praise God for his care.

46

Promise for Eternity

Do not let your hearts be troubled. You believe in God; believe also in me. My Father's house has many rooms; if that were not so, would I have told you that I am going there to prepare a place for you? And if I go and prepare a place for you, I will come back and take you to be with me that you also may be where I am.

JOHN 14:1–3

You either believe or you don't. There's no halfway. So, if you do believe in all God tells you in Scripture, in all that he promises, then you can anticipate the promise of eternity with him. But if you have even a little doubt about the truth of God's promises, you won't find much peace in them, and resting in his comfort will be difficult.

These three verses in John promise an eternal resting place that's more amazing than anything this life has to offer. Do you believe it? Do you believe that Jesus actually went to heaven to prepare a place for you? Do you trust in his promise that someday he will come for you and you will be with him? Do you trust that you will also be reunited with loved ones who have already passed from this life?

When you're grieving the loss of a loved one who also knew Jesus, take comfort in this promise that the loss is only for a while. Grief is real and it takes time to work through. That's okay. You grieve because you loved. But remember that one day you will be together again, and that will be forever!

47

Comfort of the Spirit

I will ask the Father, and he will give you another advocate to help you and be with you forever—the Spirit of truth.

JOHN 14:16–17

There are times when you feel alone. That's just part of being human. Even if you have a wonderful family, great friends, and a strong church, there may be times when you feel that others don't understand your struggle or that they don't seem to care all that much. That feeling can send you into a spiral of discouragement.

But you're not alone. Ever. Before Jesus left the earth, he made the promise you read in these verses. He knew that in your humanness you would have times of feeling like you're floating in a large ocean all alone, so he promised to ask his Father to send the Holy Spirit. He asked, God answered, and now you are never alone.

The Holy Spirit is always with you, guiding you, challenging you, and offering prayers to God on your behalf when you can't find the words. He comforts you, loves you, and celebrates with you. He is everything you need. So, when you're feeling discouraged, remember—you are not alone. The One who cares the most for you is always with you!

48

God's Daily Goodness

> *I remain confident of this:*
> *I will see the goodness of the LORD*
> *in the land of the living.*
> *Wait for the LORD;*
> *be strong and take heart*
> *and wait for the LORD.*
>
> PSALM 27:13–14

Each and every day God showers his goodness down on you because he loves you. Where do you see it? Where do God's love and comfort reach you the most?

The constancy of the sun rising every morning and setting every night speaks of God's dependability and steadiness. He is the same yesterday, today, and tomorrow.

The beauty of creation, from the vast oceans and majestic mountains and canyons to gently rolling hills, shows that he made something for everyone. In what setting do you feel closest to him?

The blessing of having loving family and friends is sometimes called God's love with skin on. He put people in your life who encourage, challenge, love, and comfort you. He shows his goodness to you through their presence in your life. The sound of a child's laughter or the hug of a grandparent—these things speak of God's love for you.

Do you see his goodness in the brilliant sunshine, the gentle rain, the powerful storm, the colors of autumn, the birth of spring? Take time this day to revel in God's goodness, whatever unique way it speaks to you. Let it remind you to take comfort in his presence with you today.

49

In Training

We know that in all things God works for the good of those who love him, who have been called according to his purpose.

ROMANS 8:28

We all want simple . . . easy . . . definite. We want to know the choices we make are the best. We don't like gray areas, and we don't enjoy indecision. We also don't want to wait. Patience is not a virtue we generally strive for. We want being a child of God to mean that he's going to cross every *t* and dot every *i* to make our lives flow smoothly. Romans 8:28 kind of promises that, doesn't it?

God loves you, that's true. God wants what is best for you—that's also true. Every day, every moment, every challenge, every situation you face is a blessing from him. Even the painful things? Even failures? Even the challenges you can't see a way out of? Yes. In every one of those situations, he is working for your good. You love him (if you're claiming this verse, don't miss that prerequisite), and he has a purpose for you. So, everything you face is part of the training to accomplish that purpose. Take comfort in that. God wastes nothing—no pain, no challenge, no failure. You're in training with the most awesome Coach!

50

Keep Doing What You Do

Therefore, my dear brothers and sisters, stand firm. Let nothing move you. Always give yourselves fully to the work of the Lord, because you know that your labor in the Lord is not in vain.

1 CORINTHIANS 15:58

Discouragement is one of Satan's biggest tools. Even some of the heroes of the Bible battled discouragement. Some thought God might have deserted them. Some felt they were the only ones left who were striving to serve God. Some grieved their own failures in obeying him. Can you identify with any of those feelings? How does Satan attack you with discouragement? Where is your weak point?

Fight against discouragement—it's Satan's tool. Don't let him win. Take comfort in the truth that the thought and energy you put into serving God—in doing whatever he has given you to do—is not wasted. Don't question each day's outcome or each person's response to your work. Just keep doing what you know to do. Obey God's guidance. Follow the direction he has given you. As long as you are doing that, you can trust that none of your work is in vain. God has a plan. He puts it together piece by piece. Your work may be only one part of it. So, don't get discouraged; be comforted that God will bless your work. Keep doing what you're doing.

51

He Forgives and Restores

From inside the fish Jonah prayed to the LORD his God. He said:

> *"In my distress I called to the LORD,*
>   *and he answered me.*
> *From deep in the realm of the dead I called for help,*
>   *and you listened to my cry."*

JONAH 2:1–2

Jonah is proof that God gives second chances. His story shows us that God forgives and restores. Have you deliberately disobeyed something God directed you to do? His direction comes as an opportunity or as a strong feeling in your gut. You *know* God wants you to do something but . . . you refuse. Have you tried to hide from God like Jonah did? Maybe you thought that if you were quiet and still then God might not notice your disobedience. That doesn't work either.

So, you disobeyed. Now what? Is the situation hopeless? No! Because no matter how far you've wandered away from him, God hears you when you cry out for another chance, and no matter how deliberately you've disobeyed him, he will give you another chance. God knows that sometimes because of fear or weakness, you will run away. But he doesn't give up on you. He loves you so very much that he will listen to your cries for help. He will forgive and restore. So don't try to hide. Instead, call out to him for help. Get back on the right path—his path! And don't forget to thank him for second chances.

52

No Man Is an Island

God, who comforts the downcast, comforted us by the coming of Titus, and not only by his coming but also by the comfort you had given him. He told us about your longing for me, your deep sorrow, your ardent concern for me, so that my joy was greater than ever.

2 Corinthians 7:6–7

Life is all about connecting with others. These verses are important because they show that the apostle Paul needed comforting and encouragement, which came through the person of Titus. Paul was also encouraged by the report that the Corinthians were concerned about him. Knowing about their concern and care comforted him and helped him to know that he wasn't alone in his struggles.

People need each other. It's encouraging to hear that others care about you and are concerned as to how your life is going. You feel less alone when you know of their prayers and concern. Encouragement from others can lift you up to face another day.

This is all in God's plan. He never intended for a person to be alone. He even told Adam, way back in the beginning, that it isn't good for man to be alone. You need people to share your life with. They give you encouragement and you give it to them. You share each other's load. No man is an island. God put you into the circle of family and friends that you have. Thank him for them and bless them with your care and comfort as you receive theirs.

53

Shout Your Gratitude

> Shout for joy, you heavens;
>   rejoice, you earth;
>   burst into song, you mountains!
> For the LORD comforts his people
>   and will have compassion on his afflicted ones.
>
> ISAIAH 49:13

When a relationship crumbles, you cry out to God for comfort. When a job loss hits, you turn to God for help. When the medical test comes back with bad news, you call on God for strength. These and many other life situations that drop you to your knees are difficult and, of course, turning to God is exactly the right thing to do. His comfort is like no other. It's deep and true and constant.

Then, the life situation improves—a new relationship, a new job, restored health, and what's your response? Perhaps a brief "thank you, God," then you get on with your life. Maybe you even shoot right to the next urgent prayer request.

Don't glide over your gratitude. The heavens shout, the earth rejoices, and even the mountains sing a song of joy because God takes care of his people . . . that means you! Celebrate his comfort. Broadcast his care. Let the whole world know that God is taking care of you. Let everyone know that he gets the credit for the comfort and care showered on you. Sing your thanks loudly!

54

Humble Yourself

Humble yourselves, therefore, under God's mighty hand, that he may lift you up in due time.

Our culture today does not encourage humility. We live in a toot-your-own-horn society where he who brags loudest and longest is the winner and where it seems the goal is not to be your best you but to be better than anyone else. Humility is viewed as weakness. But you know that's not really true.

Humbling yourself before God means you acknowledge his position and power. You confess that he is the Creator of all there is. You declare that he rules not just the universe but your life too. Remember that God is a jealous God and he insists that you humble yourself before him and allow him to be your Master. When everything around you is calling you to be proud and powerful, it's hard to be humble. When society is denying God's existence, it's not popular to let it be known you trust him.

But humbling yourself before God actually strengthens your relationship with him. The reality is that humbling yourself to him shows that your trust in him is deep. As your trust grows, your dependence on him grows, and that means his power and strength become more available to you. Trust him enough to humble yourself, and take comfort in his strength and power!

55

Worry, Worry, Worry

I, even I, am he who comforts you.
Who are you that you fear mere mortals,
human beings who are but grass?
ISAIAH 51:12

Of all the things you worry about, most of them never actually happen. But that doesn't completely stop you from worrying, does it?

What is your biggest worry? What consumes your thoughts in the middle of a dark night? Do you worry about a person who treats you badly? A bully? Maybe it's someone you have to be in contact with because of work or family relationships. You end up expending a lot of energy worrying about another person.

When you stop and think about it, you realize the foolishness of those worries. You belong to God. You are his child, and he watches over you and protects you. He guides your life and has a plan for you. Nothing and no person can disrupt God's plan because he is the most powerful. You are protected and shielded by God himself.

So while life will get difficult once in a while, God has your back, and no one will hinder God's plan. He won't allow it. That should help with your worries. Celebrate God's power and strength, which are greater than anything that causes you worry.

56

Protection in Troubled Times

In the day of trouble
*   he will keep me safe in his dwelling;*
he will hide me in the shelter of his sacred tent
*   and set me high upon a rock.*

PSALM 27:5

A small child and her mom get caught in a driving rainstorm. Mom picks up her little girl, holds her close, and wraps her own coat around the child to keep her dry as they run to safety. What a precious picture of protection. Does it help you visualize how God wraps his protection around you to cover you from the storm? He holds you close, loving you and assuring you of his presence.

An alert parent rescues a child about to take a tumble on the playground and whisks him to safety, firmly placing him in a safe place where there is no danger of falling and where he is safe. Parents are always on the lookout for their children's well-being, noticing problems and protecting against injury or danger of any kind. Children can happily run and play when they know that someone is watching out for them.

This is the protection God promises. You are not alone. Keep your trust in God, and he will protect your heart. He will calm you and give you a peace that could only come from him. Keep your heart close to him even in the midst of difficult struggles. Depend on God's comfort and protection.

57

God's Unchanging Word

Heaven and earth will pass away, but my words will never pass away.

MATTHEW 24:35

Change is hard, isn't it? When anything in life changes, there are adjustments you have to make or new things you must learn. Some change requires relocating, saying goodbye to friends and family. Even change that's good is difficult because, well, it's change.

In a world where things change by the minute, it's nice to know there is something that will never change. God's Word will always be God's Word. It is never going away. The inspired words of the Bible that you have studied and memorized will always be true. The principles on which you have based your life will always be truth. Nothing will be taken away from those truths and no new truth is being revealed. Everything else in this world may change, but God's Word will remain the same.

Take comfort in this fact. God promises that you can trust his Word. So, read it, study it, know it, and pray it. Then even if the world declares new revelations about what God says or means, you can talk directly with God and he will clarify the truth of his unchanging Word. His Spirit will speak truth into your mind about the Scriptures you have studied.

58

Money, Money, Money!

Blessed are those who find wisdom,
those who gain understanding,
for she is more profitable than silver
and yields better returns than gold.
PROVERBS 3:13–14

Everyone wants money! Getting more and more of it is the passion of far too many people. Our culture insists that those with the most money are the winners. Those who buy in to this belief spend pretty much all their time working, growing their career, and striving for a bigger salary. There's nothing wrong with having a successful career or doing well financially. But if pursuing that becomes more important than knowing God and spending time with him, then you have a problem.

Make it your focus to study God's Word, and let it sink into your heart so that it becomes the standard by which you live—then take comfort in the fact that you have found wisdom. You have made the right choice. It is a sign of maturity to keep your priorities focused on knowing and serving God and understanding his Word. The blessing of doing this is more rewarding than having all the money in the world or all the success that money can buy.

Thank God for his Word and for the wisdom you gain by knowing it and spending time with him. Find comfort and grace in the blessing of your choice to honor him.

59

True Success

> *The Lord said to Samuel, "Do not consider his appearance or his height, for I have rejected him. The Lord does not look at the things people look at. People look at the outward appearance, but the Lord looks at the heart."*
>
> 1 SAMUEL 16:7

Most of the time the comparison game leaves you feeling that you come up short. Someone else's appearance might make you feel like you need to lose weight or gain weight or like you need a new hairstyle or new clothes. Your career compared to another's seems to show only failures. The comparison monster attacks your feelings about your house, your decorating ability, your talents, your children's abilities . . . it can hit anywhere, and it is never good.

Why do you hold yourself up next to another and allow that comparison to make you feel less than? It's not true. You are who you are and you have what you have because that's how God made you and where God put you. Can you work at developing and growing your skills and improving your appearance by taking care of yourself? Sure, do that. But then realize that God doesn't care as much about those things as people do. He looks at your heart to see if you are submitted to him. He cares about whether you are loving and caring toward others. Take comfort in this: God looks at your heart and you should too. Success comes from a heart devoted to him.

60

No Bragging

Therefore, whoever takes the lowly position of this child is the greatest in the kingdom of heaven.

MATTHEW 18:4

Maybe you know someone (hopefully it's not you) who wants to be the center of attention. Someone who toots their own horn by pointing out their success and status in life. Instead of lifting others up, this person often self-promotes and wants recognition for how important they are. Whew. That kind of person is tiring to be around. Life is always about them and never about others.

If you're one of the people this braggart shoves down so that they appear more important, don't feel bad about yourself. Take comfort in this statement from Jesus. He pointed at a child—a young child who had not yet accomplished great things in life—and he said that this child is the greatest in heaven. Why? Because children show humbleness before God. Since most children have not yet known great successes in life, they look to God as their Master. Their hearts are blank slates, open to learning all that God will teach them. Be comforted that as you stand before God, not bragging and self-promoting, but with a heart open to learning and guiding, you are a success in his eyes.

61

Private Conversation

The LORD is near to all who call on him,
to all who call on him in truth.

PSALM 145:18

Imagine an adult and a small child are having a conversation. The child speaks softly, so the adult bends down and inclines her ear toward him so she can better hear him speak. She even covers her other ear so she can concentrate on that small child. Their faces are close together because that child has her full attention.

Now imagine God doing that with you. Prayer is such a privilege. Think about it: the Creator and Ruler of everything there is—God, the most powerful, strong, creative, and just Being—wants to hear from you. God cares, and he invites you to tell him what's on your heart. He wants to know what you care about. He promises to draw close to you so he can hear your prayers.

You can tell God what's worrying you, what you're afraid of, what concerns you. You can tell him your hopes, wishes, and dreams. You can ask for his help, guidance, and strength. You can tell him *anything* because he loves you. His ear is leaning in close to hear your whispered words.

62

Always Good

Give thanks to the LORD, for he is good;
his love endures forever.
1 CHRONICLES 16:34

Have you ever been disappointed by a person you thought you knew pretty well? It hurts, doesn't it? Maybe it was a friend or family member whose character you thought you knew well and whose behavior you thought you could anticipate. When that person acts totally opposite of what you expect, it's disappointing and hurtful.

You will never face that kind of disappointment with God. He will always be true to his character. He cannot be any other way. You don't have to wonder if God will suddenly turn selfish, cranky, mean, or vindictive—he won't. God is always good, and he loves you completely and unconditionally. He always will. You cannot do anything to change that. If you fail him, he will still love you. If you deliberately disobey him, he will still love you. If you doubt him, he will still love you.

What a comfort this is, because, of course, there will be times when you disobey. There will be times when you doubt. There will be times when you question. But nothing you do will stop God from loving you. He is good. He loves you. Thank him for that.

63

Training Manual

All Scripture is God-breathed and is useful for teaching, rebuking, correcting and training in righteousness, so that the servant of God may be thoroughly equipped for every good work.

2 TIMOTHY 3:16–17

When you start a new job the training period can last up to a couple of months, depending on how complicated the job is. It's an important time for you to learn the details of the job and to be sure you can handle in the best possible way any situation that may come up. Sometimes the company even has a manual that you need to study so that you can perform your job according to company standards and in a way that is compatible with your coworkers.

As you grow in your relationship with Christ, there will be times when you have questions about how to be obedient to God, how to serve him, and how to relate to other people. Those questions are all answered in Scripture. In the Bible, God tells you what obedience looks like. He also tells you how you can serve him and how you should treat others. When you read in the Bible about how God has interacted with his people throughout history, you learn about his character.

God's comfort, character, and guidance wait for you in the pages of your Bible. It's the best training manual for living with God!

64

One Step Forward . . .

Do not be anxious about anything, but in every situation, by prayer and petition, with thanksgiving, present your requests to God. And the peace of God, which transcends all understanding, will guard your hearts and your minds in Christ Jesus.

PHILIPPIANS 4:6–7

It takes a lot of mental and spiritual energy to worry, and that energy could certainly be better spent on something else. But it's hard to turn worry off. So, what do you do? How do you stop worry? Here's the formula: give every worry to God. Regardless of what is tying your stomach in knots, ask God to take care of it. Thank him for handling it—even before he has done a thing. That shows your faith in him.

Then you're good, right? You trust God. You stop worrying. You have peace. Well, sometimes this is a one step forward, two steps back kind of process. So, take it a step at a time. Take your requests to God. Try to leave your concerns there with him. When you're successful with that, enjoy the peace it brings. The last phrase of these verses is important— ask God to guard your heart so that you are able to leave your worries with him and enjoy the peace he gives.

65

Confidence in God

This is the confidence we have in approaching God: that if we ask anything according to his will, he hears us. And if we know that he hears us—whatever we ask—we know that we have what we asked of him.

1 John 5:14–15

It's comforting to know you can have confidence in someone. There is so much uncertainty in this life that it's a relief to know that you can always feel confident with God because he will always do what he says.

However, the promise that he will hear your prayer and give you what you ask for is not a way to get whatever you want from him. The four little words in the middle of this promise are the key—*according to his will*. Ask him anything you want, and as long as it's according to his will, he will give you what you ask for.

This isn't a trick—it's not an impossible condition. When you are in constant contact with God by spending time in his Word and talking with him, you begin to pray according to his will. You begin to want the same things he wants for you. You want to serve him and obey him. Then the things you pray for are what he wants to give you. If you do pray for something that isn't in his will, you can take comfort in the truth that he has your best interest in mind.

66

Red Rover!

No temptation has overtaken you except what is common to mankind. And God is faithful; he will not let you be tempted beyond what you can bear. But when you are tempted, he will also provide a way out so that you can endure it.

1 CORINTHIANS 10:13

Temptation is part of life. You may think you're strong enough to resist it, but even that thought is caused by the temptation to have pride in your own strength. When push comes to shove, Satan knows which temptations will be too much for you to resist on your own. He's crafty and will keep placing that pretty temptation in front of you, hoping that you can't resist.

But you're not alone! God sees the temptations the evil one slides in front of you and knows when you are at your limit. That's when he steps in. God will help you fight against Satan's attacks.

God may not completely remove the temptation, but he will help you resist it. He will open your eyes to a way around it, and he will give you strength to keep pushing it back. Remember the child's game Red Rover? You joined hands with a friend and held tightly as an opponent tried to break through. God becomes your Red Rover partner and Satan cannot break through. What a victory that is! Each time you resist him, you know that it's because God is fighting for you and with you. You are not alone in the battle!

67

Really Living

Then Jesus said to his disciples, "Whoever wants to be my disciple must deny themselves and take up their cross and follow me. For whoever wants to save their life will lose it, but whoever loses their life for me will find it."

MATTHEW 16:24–25

In your opinion, what's the mark of a life well lived? Does it involve climbing the success ladder or accumulating loads of money? Is it having the most power, the biggest house, or the newest car? Some people consider those things to be the standards for success. Those opinions may be what you're up against if you have chosen to devote your life to Jesus. Your measurement of success becomes his, which is based on humility and service.

People around you who aren't Jesus's followers may be critical of your choices, feeling that you're wasting your potential. Even if they don't say it, you can sense their judgmental opinion.

Don't let others' opinions discourage you because, in the important picture of all eternity, you have made exactly the right choice. Giving your life completely over to Jesus, so that your main focus is to follow and obey him, means that you have truly found your life. Others may not understand it, but serving Jesus by serving others—giving of your time, finances, energy, or attention—truly matters. Sharing your faith with others so that they may know him is what matters most. Jesus said it . . . you have found true life.

68

Go Forward
with Confidence

Be strong and courageous. Do not be afraid; do not be discouraged, for the LORD your God will be with you wherever you go.

JOSHUA 1:9

Have you been through one of those dark times when it feels as though God is so distant you can't reach him even with your most sincere prayers? Life presses down on you to the point that getting out of bed is an effort, and getting out of your pajamas is an impossibility. It feels as though you're alone with no friends and no support system. It's scary. No, it's terrifying. Has God really deserted you? Are you free-floating through life, an open target for your enemies?

Sometimes it feels as though God sort of pulls back from you. Maybe it's an opportunity to stretch your faith muscle. You must really lean on the truth that God has promised to be with you wherever you go. Always. Without a doubt. No matter what.

Whatever you're going through . . . whatever you're feeling . . . trust God's promise that you are not alone. He is with you, which means his strength and power are fighting for you. His love is surrounding you. You're not an open target for evil. Go forward with that confidence.

69

No Longer Alienated

Once you were alienated from God and were enemies in your minds because of your evil behavior. But now he has reconciled you by Christ's physical body through death to present you holy in his sight, without blemish and free from accusation.

COLOSSIANS 1:21–22

Alienation means there is no relationship. It usually means you have no contact, no conversation with the person from whom you are alienated. If you feel that the broken relationship was caused by something you did, then it's even worse. Maybe you don't know how to fix it, so you just continue on with no contact with that person.

Before you accept Jesus as your Savior, you have that kind of alienation from God—no personal relationship, no connection, no friendship, no communication. The solution has already been provided; you just may not know it yet. What's amazing is that you don't have to do a thing to provide the solution for your alienation from God. He does everything. All you have to do is accept it.

Now, because of Jesus's sacrifice, by the grace of God he sees you as holy. Did you read that right? Yes, holy in his sight. You are set apart from your past. No scars. No blemishes at all. No filth. He sees you as snow white, free from any accusations directed at you. Praise God for his complete, unconditional forgiveness. All you have to do is accept it.

70

God's Comforter

If Christ is in you, then even though your body is subject to death because of sin, the Spirit gives life because of righteousness. And if the Spirit of him who raised Jesus from the dead is living in you, he who raised Christ from the dead will also give life to your mortal bodies because of his Spirit who lives in you.

ROMANS 8:10–11

We don't talk much about the Holy Spirit, but we should—he is the power of God within you. Remember that when Jesus was preparing to return to heaven he promised to ask his Father to send One called a "Helper" or an "Advocate" or "Counselor." That is the Holy Spirit.

Whether your life is stuck in the day-in and day-out boredom of sameness or whether you are facing big changes that bring brand-new stresses, the Spirit reminds you that you're not alone.

Remember it was the power of the Holy Spirit that raised Jesus from the dead. That's some awesome power . . . and it's that same power that gives you the strength to put one foot in front of the other and keep on going when you don't have the strength on your own. It's his power that gives your tired mind wisdom and your aching heart patience. His presence in your heart affirms that one day things will be better and that you are never, ever alone on your journey. The Spirit's work helps you know God more fully, trust him more completely, and love him more deeply. He is God's special gift to you.

71

Living a Godly Life

His divine power has given us everything we need for a godly life through our knowledge of him who called us by his own glory and goodness. Through these he has given us his very great and precious promises, so that through them you may participate in the divine nature, having escaped the corruption in the world caused by evil desires.

2 PETER 1:3–4

In the days before email, people only heard from far-away loved ones via an actual handwritten letter. What a joy to receive that long-awaited communication and read of your loved one's activities, thoughts, and feelings. People treasured those letters, often reading them over and over. God's Word . . . his Bible . . . is his letter to you.

Through his Word, God gives you everything you need to know to focus your behavior on becoming more and more godly. His Word acts as a mirror to show you where you're falling short in godly behavior. It gives you the guidelines to strive to incorporate into your life. It shows you what God expects of you. God also promises in his Word that his strength and power are available to you. They will help you in your growth to live a godly life. It's not something you have to do on your own. In fact, you can't possibly do it without God's power, strength, patience, love, and guidance. Those things are just what he promises when you read his Word, memorize it, and claim his promises.

72

Keeping Focus

*Those who hope in the L*ord
will renew their strength.
They will soar on wings like eagles;
they will run and not grow weary,
they will walk and not be faint.

Isaiah 40:31

competitive gymnast stands on a four-inch-wide balance beam, twirls a few times on one foot, then jumps into a split-leg jump and lands . . . balanced sturdily on the beam. How does she keep from getting so dizzy in those twirls that she can't land balanced on the four-inch-wide beam? She keeps her focus. Before she begins the twirls, she focuses on something straight ahead of her and stays focused on it so each time she twirls past it, she knows where she is.

Growing in your faith-walk takes focus too. There will be things and people every day that try to make you fall. Keep your eyes on Jesus. Scripture says he is the Pioneer and Perfecter of your faith (see Heb. 12:2). So as you go through life, stay close to him by talking with him daily and reading his Word. Meditate on it so it sinks down into your heart. Learn from it as your faith-walk grows deeper. Your reward for that focus is the strength, perseverance, and energy promised in this verse. You can face anything if you stay focused on Jesus.

73

Strength in Numbers

Two are better than one,
*   because they have a good return for their labor:*
If either of them falls down,
*   one can help the other up.*

ECCLESIASTES 4:9–10

Your friends and family are important! They give you encouragement to keep going by giving you a pat on the back and telling you "good job" or "way to go." They give accountability, calling into question choices you make that seem to veer away from who you really are, making you stop and think about what you're doing. They offer rescue, helping you when you have too much on your plate or don't have the strength to put one foot in front of the other, or by simply offering to pray for you. They help with strength, standing with you and saying, "together we can fight this," when someone is discouraging you and beating you down.

God has put people in your life for a reason—don't push them away; embrace them. Accept their comfort and strength. Allow them to help you, and then be willing to help them when necessary. They are present for you and you are present for them, especially those who share your faith in God. You can help one another stand firm for him. There's strength in numbers and God knows that.

74

No Pain, No Gain

We also glory in our sufferings, because we know that suffering produces perseverance; perseverance, character; and character, hope. And hope does not put us to shame, because God's love has been poured out into our hearts through the Holy Spirit, who has been given to us.

ROMANS 5:3–5

Making the effort to get healthy usually involves exercise of some kind. Exercise often results in a tired body and sore muscles. It's challenging to continue putting your body through that pain, but you know that it's progressing you toward a healthier body. It fulfills the "no pain, no gain" rally cry of true athletes.

How does that rally cry match up with the Christian life? The reality is that tough things happen in life. And tough things cause suffering. What's your response to the pain of suffering? Can you see it as part of the process that is building and strengthening your spiritual muscles? Can you see that it's preparing you for even greater struggles that might be ahead?

When you face struggles, take comfort in the truth that they are part of the process of teaching you to keep fighting through the tough times. That perseverance helps you develop your character so you can become more like Christ. Becoming more like Christ helps you remember that you operate within the depths of God's love and the power of the Holy Spirit. That helps you face more tough times. That's the cycle. Now do you see the value of "no pain, no gain"?

75

Calling to God

*Ask and it will be given to you; seek and you will find; knock
and the door will be opened to you. For everyone who asks re-
ceives; the one who seeks finds; and to the one who knocks, the
door will be opened.*

MATTHEW 7:7–8

If you have children or have even been around children,
you have probably heard the constant, "Mom. Mom.
Mom. Mommy. Mom." Children have incredible perseverance to keep calling out until their mother finally answers.
Moms of persistent children tend to learn a little bit of selec-
tive hearing.

Thankfully, you don't have to keep calling God's name
over and over to get his attention. You can come straight to
him and make your requests. He's always available to you.
He is always listening. Does this mean that you can ask for
whatever you want? "God, give me a million dollars!" "God,
take away my problems!" That would be so easy, wouldn't it?

But it's not what these verses mean. God is not some celestial Santa Claus waiting to give you whatever you want.

The key to these verses is your relationship with Christ. The closer you are to him, the more your desires mirror his desires for you. Then, your requests become exactly what he wants for you. You won't need to constantly call his name. As you grow closer to him, seeking him, then you will understand even more what his will is for you.

76

Real Wisdom

But the Advocate, the Holy Spirit, whom the Father will send in my name, will teach you all things and will remind you of everything I have said to you. Peace I leave with you; my peace I give you. I do not give to you as the world gives. Do not let your hearts be troubled and do not be afraid.

John 14:26–27

Do you sometimes feel like you're floating through life with no guidance or direction—somewhat like a soap bubble floating aimlessly?

You don't need to feel that way. God made sure of that. When Jesus left the earth, he asked the Father to send the Holy Spirit to believers to be their Advocate. The Holy Spirit is also called the Counselor and the Comforter. The Spirit lives in your heart and reminds you of all that Jesus taught his followers. He reminds you what Scripture teaches about obeying God and serving him. He convicts you when you aren't obeying, and he guides you in your decisions. He doesn't do any of this in anger or judgment; he does it because he loves you and wants the best for you. He even prays for you when you are so distraught or confused that you simply can't find the words to pray.

The Spirit/Advocate/Counselor/Comforter is God's gift to you so that you may have peace based on your relationship with God. Your trust and dependence on the Father grows deeper and stronger as you learn from the Spirit's guidance in your heart and obey his challenges to follow God's teachings.

77

Jesus Came in Love

*God did not send his Son into the world to condemn the world,
but to save the world through him.*

JOHN 3:17

When you were in school were you ever sent to the principal's office for behavior issues? Or did you ever fear that happening? It's pretty intimidating to face a person of authority when you know you have misbehaved and will be punished. Even if you haven't done something wrong but a person of authority calls you in, nerves flutter in your stomach.

Jesus didn't come into the world to judge people. He came in love to teach about God and to explain how to live for him and how to live in community with other people. Jesus came to save the world, not to condemn it. You don't need to fear him as you might a person in authority. His coming is based in love.

Look at all Jesus did in his ministry on earth: He healed sick people, gave sight to the blind, raised the dead back to life. He forgave people buried in sin. He cared about people, and he showed that through his teachings and his actions. He cares about you too. No matter what is weighing you down, he cares. He will help. He will comfort. Just ask him.

78

Discipline Time

*My son, do not despise the Lord's discipline,
and do not resent his rebuke,
because the Lord disciplines those he loves,
as a father the son he delights in.*

Proverbs 3:11–12

I t's no fun to be disciplined. You can probably recall a time when your parents disciplined you. You may have resented it at the time, but as you matured you realized that discipline from someone who loves you is actually for the purpose of teaching and training. It helps you become a responsible adult who contributes to society and to the lives of others. If you have children you also realize the responsibility that comes with disciplining and that it isn't fun for the parent either.

God's discipline is also for the purpose of teaching and training. His discipline may take the form of sitting you down through injury or illness to slow you down, or it may be in something being taken away for a while. Remember that he wouldn't discipline you if he didn't love you. His ultimate goal for you is that you become more like Christ in your humility and submission to him and in the compassionate way you interact with others. His discipline helps you keep your focus. Love God, love others. Sometimes you need disciplinary pruning in your life for that to happen. Don't resent it. Thank him for it. He's doing it to teach you because he loves you.

79

What's Your Job?

Christ himself gave the apostles, the prophets, the evangelists, the pastors and teachers, to equip his people for works of service, so that the body of Christ may be built up until we all reach unity in the faith and in the knowledge of the Son of God and become mature, attaining to the whole measure of the fullness of Christ.

EPHESIANS 4:11–13

Perhaps you've seen the children's toys that are various shaped pieces of plastic, each covered with plastic bristles. You can press the pieces together and build things. When fitted together, the individual pieces become more than just one single piece; together they make something. Each piece is necessary to create the finished product.

This is much like God's kingdom. God has given each believer gifts of talents and abilities. He has also placed in each person's heart compassion for unique situations or people groups. He has done that for you. The talents and heart yearnings that are in you are necessary to his work on this earth. Your work is neither more nor less important than anyone else's. It is what God has called you to do. When you accept Christ, you become important to people around you who don't know the Lord. Through your life and words, you have the opportunity to show them the love of God. You can care for fellow believers by encouraging them to grow deeper in their faith.

What a privilege you have to share in the work of God! Your obedience in serving God is important for two reasons: it's what he wants you to do, and it's important to the purpose of sharing his love with others. Give it your best!

80

Real Peace

A heart at peace gives life to the body,
but envy rots the bones.

PROVERBS 14:30

Everyone wants peace. Few people actually have it. Being at peace means that you accept life as it comes. You aren't filled with angst about what you don't have or can't do or about situations that you have no control over. A heart at peace accepts that God is in control and believes that whatever his plan is . . . it is good.

What's a roadblock to having a heart at peace? Envy is certainly one of those things. A heart filled with envy is always looking around at what others have that you don't have or what they can do that you can't do and thinking that those things could make your life so much better. No peace will come from that attitude. A heart at peace doesn't compare; it accepts. It doesn't make cynical (jealous) comments about the things that others do.

If you have a peaceful heart, your attitude toward others is healthy and supportive. You can focus your energy on doing what you're good at and enjoying what you have. You're in a good place. Thank God for your peaceful heart that is submitted to him and for rewarding you with a peaceful life.

81

Do Love

Let love and faithfulness never leave you;
bind them around your neck,
write them on the tablet of your heart.
Then you will win favor and a good name
in the sight of God and man.

PROVERBS 3:3–4

Do you know why God so often tells you to love others? Because it makes a difference. You can probably think of someone in your circle of friends who is really good at love, kindness, and compassion. She is a delight to be around, isn't she? She brings joy and comfort.

How do you live out love in everyday life? You probably do it often without even thinking about it. You probably receive it often too. It comes through smiling at a stranger, holding a door open, speaking a kind word, picking up something someone unknowingly dropped.

You could take it to the next level by going out of your way to hand a bottle of water to someone or by playing with a child so an exhausted mom has time to do a chore. Maybe you could spend time talking with someone who is lonely or give a word of encouragement.

These simple things and many other actions are love and comfort to those who receive them as well as to those who give them. Intentionally live in love so that you are God's comfort to those around you, and receive his comfort from those he has put in your life.

82

Completely Clean

> *"Come now, let us settle the matter,"*
>   *says the Lord.*
> *"Though your sins are like scarlet,*
>   *they shall be as white as snow;*
> *though they are red as crimson,*
>   *they shall be like wool."*
>
> Isaiah 1:18

Red ink, blood, red paint . . . those are difficult stains to get out of fabric. Almost impossible, even with our miracle-working laundry products. Red may fade to pink, but the stain is still visible. That's why it's interesting that God uses red as the color to describe sin. Obviously he could be referring to the red color of blood, as that's what was required as the sacrifice for sin. But as a busy woman who does lots of laundry and cleaning, think about the comparison. Red—especially on a white fabric—stands out. Red is hard to erase. Red will fade but will not go completely away. So the evidence of the stain is always visible, even to the naked eye.

That's how visible your sin would be to God without Jesus's sacrifice paving the way for God's forgiveness. Look at what God did—he wiped all evidence of your sin away! No matter what you've done, by God's grace, he has forgiven you and cleansed you with no evidence of the stain of your sin.

How loving and kind your God is! When you ask his forgiveness, he forgives and you are clean in his eyes.

83

The Blessings of Today

Rejoice always, pray continually, give thanks in all circumstances; for this is God's will for you in Christ Jesus.

1 Thessalonians 5:16–18

Life is a journey. There will be some hard times, but you will make it through them. There will be some wonderful times that you celebrate. There will be some normal, everyday, not-hard-but-not-great times—in fact, that may be most of your days.

The joy of life is to celebrate each and every day. Find the blessings of God's work in your life. Notice his blessings, and realize that some of them come in the form of difficulties that draw you closer to him.

Quiet your heart each day. Slow down and be still so you have time to rejoice in God's presence in your life. Pay attention to the ways he reveals himself to you. Rejoice in the now. Notice and celebrate the everyday blessings of a child's hug, a friend's smile, a beautiful flower, or whatever brings you joy. Thank God for all things—the difficult, painful things you face and the wonderful, joyous things too. Rejoicing in them and thanking God for them brings you into the moment so you can see the glorious blessings of God in each day!

84

Wonderful You

For you created my inmost being;
you knit me together in my mother's womb.
I praise you because I am fearfully and wonderfully
made;
your works are wonderful,
I know that full well.

PSALM 139:13–14

Everything your body needed to become a full-grown adult was knitted together by God while you were still in your mother's womb. What a miracle!

No doubt when you were born your parents had wonderful hopes and dreams for you to have a blessed and joy-filled life. God did too! God saw you before you were born. He planned your hair color, your eye color, and how tall you would be. He chose which talents and gifts he would grace you with. He chose whether you would be athletic or musical or both. He planned whether you would be funny, serious, or thoughtful—he planned you! He knew what career you'd choose and whether you would marry.

God sees every day of your life from your birth to your death. And yes, he made you just the way he wants you to be, and you are wonderful! If you face challenges, he will use those to strengthen you and to bless others in amazing ways. He will teach you and others through your struggles. God doesn't make mistakes. He makes blessings. He makes lessons. He makes miracles. Celebrate you!

85

Vine and Branches

I am the vine; you are the branches. If you remain in me and I in you, you will bear much fruit; apart from me you can do nothing.

JOHN 15:5

There is great comfort in this verse because it is evidence that you don't have to push through this life on your own. You don't have to try to serve God in your own power and strength. In fact, if you try to do that, you will most certainly fail.

Jesus's example of a plant is so good because the vine of a plant delivers the nourishment to the whole plant. The roots draw food and water from the soil and are connected to the vine. The vine delivers the nourishment to the branches so they can be healthy. The vine of the plant is the heart of the plant. Jesus is the Vine for you. If you stay connected to him through Bible reading and prayer time, your heart will be nourished and fed. Your faith will grow stronger. But if you cut yourself off from him, you will die spiritually just as a branch cut from a plant dies without nourishment.

Stay connected to Jesus. Let him nourish you. Grow strong and healthy in your service to God. You're not in this life alone.

86

Love Deeply

Above all, love each other deeply, because love covers over a multitude of sins.

1 PETER 4:8

ove each other. That sounds so simple, doesn't it? What could be easier than loving? But it isn't easy . . . at least not with some people . . . at least not all the time. Some people take advantage of you or think only of themselves. How do you love them deeply? It's important to actually love, not just to talk about loving. If you love someone deeply, then you love with actions as well as words. If you love enough to cover over a multitude of sins, then you're loving sacrificially. You're letting go of your own needs and agenda, and you're realizing that people aren't perfect (neither are you). Sometimes people can love you the way you need to be loved, and sometimes they can't. So you're willing to overlook their failures, recognize their good intentions, and give them another chance.

Your action of forgiving and loving someone after their failure may open the door for them to be able to do better the next time. After all, God forgives and loves and forgives and loves over and over again. Reflect his love to others and love them deeply and sacrificially.

87

Pay It Forward

We love because he first loved us.
1 John 4:19

What could your response to God's love be except to pay it forward and to love those around you? You've probably heard that phrase, "Pay it forward." You hear of someone paying for the coffee of the person behind them in line at a coffee shop or of someone paying the road toll for the car behind them at a toll booth—just showing generosity and love for no reason except to be kind. It is encouraging to know there is still love and kindness in this crazy world.

How do *you* do it? How do you pay forward God's love to the world around you? It has to be with actions, not just words. Jesus loved with actions by healing sick people and raising the dead. Yes, he taught, too, but he backed up his teaching with actions. He "did" love. He still does. He does love with you. What's your favorite way God shows his love to you? The steady ocean waves? Regal mountains? The hug of a child? Kind words from a friend? A beautiful song? He loves you in many ways every day. What's your response? Notice and receive his love, then pay it forward to those you come in contact with each day.

88

What Love Does

When Jesus landed and saw a large crowd, he had compassion on them, because they were like sheep without a shepherd. So he began teaching them many things.

MARK 6:34

This is one verse among many about how Jesus related to people. He got out of a boat after crossing a huge lake. It had been a long day, and he was probably tired. Jesus was always surrounded by people who wanted something from him. Maybe he wanted to be alone or to go rest somewhere. But he got out of that boat and saw people who didn't know God, people who didn't have someone to follow, people who needed what Jesus could give. So, in compassion, tired as he must have been, he taught them about God. Not only did he teach them, he multiplied fish and loaves of bread to feed over five thousand of them! It mattered to Jesus that these people hear about God's love. And he knew they wouldn't really be able to focus on his words if their stomachs were growling.

He still shows that deep compassion every day . . . to you. He loves you, so when he sees you hurting, he makes sure you are comforted. When he sees that you need guidance, he makes sure you get it. He takes care of you. That's what love does. Do you see it? Do you recognize his compassion poured out on you?

89

Build a Team

Carry each other's burdens, and in this way you will fulfill the law of Christ.

GALATIANS 6:2

Have you ever played tug-of-war? Two teams of people grab on to opposite ends of a rope, and the goal of the game is for one team to pull the other team across a center line. The team that is successful wins. It's a fun game, but the important factor is that the team members must work together to pull. Their timing must be coordinated. Their ability to work together will win the game.

Teamwork—what a grand concept! Having a team of people around you makes life so much easier. When you have a problem or a concern, you can share it with your team-mates, and together you can talk about it and pray over it. You carry the load of that problem together. The weight of it is shared among you and your team of people. It's God's plan that you do that for each other. Your team of friends share your load so you aren't defeated by your problems. This creates community. Having relationships, loving each other, caring for each other, helping each other—that's what God wants for his children. So don't hide your burdens from your team; share them.

90

Love Your Enemies

Your love, LORD, reaches to the heavens,
your faithfulness to the skies.
Your righteousness is like the highest mountains,
your justice like the great deep.
You, LORD, preserve both people and animals.

PSALM 36:5–6

Life is made up of hours, days, weeks, months, and years. Some seasons of life present moment-by-moment challenges. Some seasons are joy-filled celebrations. God is in every single one of those seasons. He is always with you. He never turns aside or looks away, because he loves you so much.

God's love is beyond human comprehension. As these verses say, it reaches to the farthest star you can see . . . and beyond. He is as dependable as the sky's presence. His justice and righteousness are bigger than any image you can think of.

God is paying attention to every moment of your life, but he won't force his way into your life. He waits for you to seek him out. He guides and protects and cares for you in ways that you may not even notice. He cares so much for you that he gave you his Word to help you learn about him and to show his love in action, he gave you his Spirit to guide your heart, and he put people around you to encourage and help you.

God's love is big, powerful, and constant, and there is nothing he will not do for you!

Carolyn Larsen is the bestselling author of more than fifty books for children and adults. She has been a speaker for women's events and classes around the world, bringing scriptural messages filled with humor and tenderness. For more information, visit carolynlarsen.com and follow her on Facebook.

Connect with
Carolyn

Author Photo: Bennorth Images of St. Charles, IL

CAROLYNLARSEN.COM

 Carolyn Larsen

Find *Hope* through the Promises in God's Word

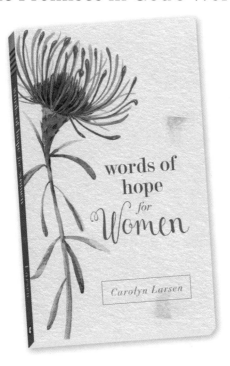

words of
hope
for
Women

Carolyn Larsen

A 90-day devotional that encourages you during the challenges of life, offering hope through the promises in God's Word and the people he places in your path.

 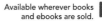